A loving tribute to my son, Steven Charles Archer.
~Phyllis Hall

This book is dedicated to those
who are learning the strength of love,
whether separated for
an hour or a lifetime.

*With appreciation to all of my friends and family who helped me make this book possible.*

Limited Edition of 2000

*Mother of Angels*

Published by Mother of Angels
300 Carlsbad Village Drive
Suite 108 A #84
Carlsbad, CA 92008
760-434-5683 (LOVE)

ISBN 0-9717770-0-4
PCN 2002100211

Printed in China

# With Me Always

By Phyllis Hall
Illustrated By Bonnie Bright

Every night a happy-hearted angel named Moonbeam is busy in the heavens above. It is Moonbeam's job to make sure that all the stars in the moon's beam are polished and clean, so that even the tiniest star shines. This is a very important position in heaven, because these shining stars light the path for new angels to follow home at night.

One night Moonbeam noticed a young couple gazing up at the sky. Their eyes were filled with the wonder of love. Moonbeam wanted to help their love grow, so that night the angel worked even harder. Moonbeam smiled as they shared a first kiss under the shining stars.

Many nights later under the brilliant sky, the young man asked the young woman to become his wife.   The following year they were married in their special spot under the stars.  Moonbeam watched happily from above, and all the little stars twinkled brightly.

The years passed by quickly for the young couple. They were happy, but their hearts yearned for a child. One night the young woman went alone to their special spot and looked up at the heavens. "We would like a child to love," she said out loud, and as she spoke, she began to cry.

Then the young woman heard a voice. It was Moonbeam telling her good news. "You will be given a child for awhile, but you'll love him forever, my dear," said the angel. "Oh, that is wonderful!" the young woman exclaimed. "But why for only awhile?" she asked. The angel was silent.

Her tears came faster then, and because they were filled with hope and happiness now, they began to beam with light.  As they fell and hit the ground, they sparkled and flew like little fireflies. The young woman twirled around in circles as the lights danced at her feet.

When she stopped, she looked down and saw to her amazement,

a beautiful baby lying in a blanket.  Her heart filled with love.

She quickly picked up her brand new baby and said, "You're a

gift from an angel's heart.  I will name you Angelheart!"

Elephant

Little Angelheart lived joyfully

with this very special couple.  They loved

their precious child, and watched him closely as he

grew from a baby to a toddler and then on through childhood.

The days and years passed quickly and were filled with

adventure and fun.

The little family cherished every laugh and every happy time together.

They celebrated every birthday by having Angelheart's most favorite

dinner, a juicy cheeseburger and a chocolate milkshake!

One night after a birthday celebration, Angelheart asked his parents to walk to their special spot under the stars. "Look up," Angelheart said. "Remember when you first met, and how the stars seemed to shine so brilliantly? That was because my guardian angel, Moonbeam, worked extra hard to shine all those pretty stars, so that your love would grow and grow."

"Moonbeam told me many secrets on the night I was born," Angelheart continued.  " I learned that I would only have a little time to be with you because someday I would be needed to help polish the stars.  I told Moonbeam it was better to be with you for awhile, than to have no time at all."

"If the stars don't get polished, they'll soon go out," he explained. "It is my special job to help keep them bright forever. I've been blessed to be with you, but now I must help to polish the stars and brighten the path for new angels."

Then Angelheart said, "I have something special I want to give you." He opened his hands. His parents gasped in wonder at the radiant gold angel heart that lay in his palms. "I have always kept this close as a reminder that I have a guardian angel who loves me. Now I want you to have it as a symbol of our love. It will remind you that I am with you always, in your heart, just like you're in mine."

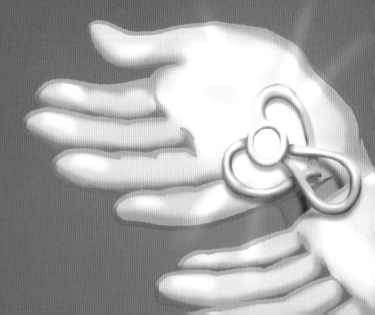

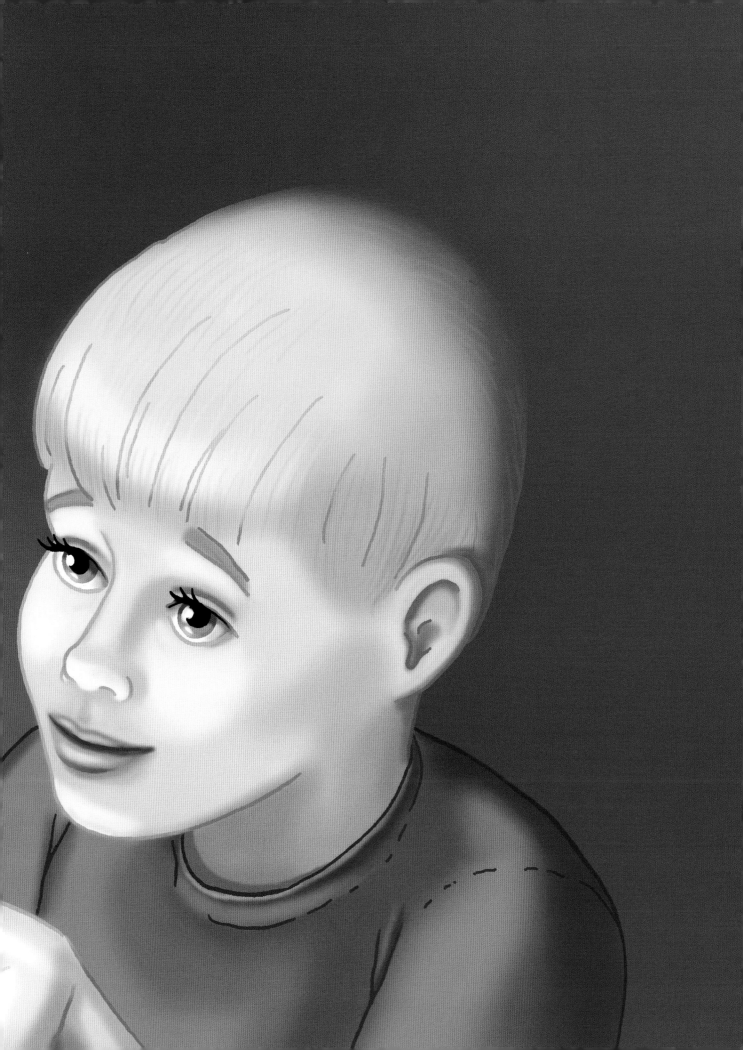

Angelheart's parents knew that they would miss him, but they understood that the stars needed to shine. They were quite proud that he had been given such a very important job.  With a smile they gave him a great big hug, but their eyes were filled with tears. The tears dropped all around them, and as they did, like once before, each one turned into a little light that sparkled and flew like a firefly.

The lights flew in circles, and some landed in a bucket that was lying on the ground. Angelheart's mother picked it up and said, "Please, take this bucket of special tears with you. We want you to use them to make the stars shine even brighter so new angels can find their way." Angelheart took the flickering bucket and kissed them both on their foreheads.

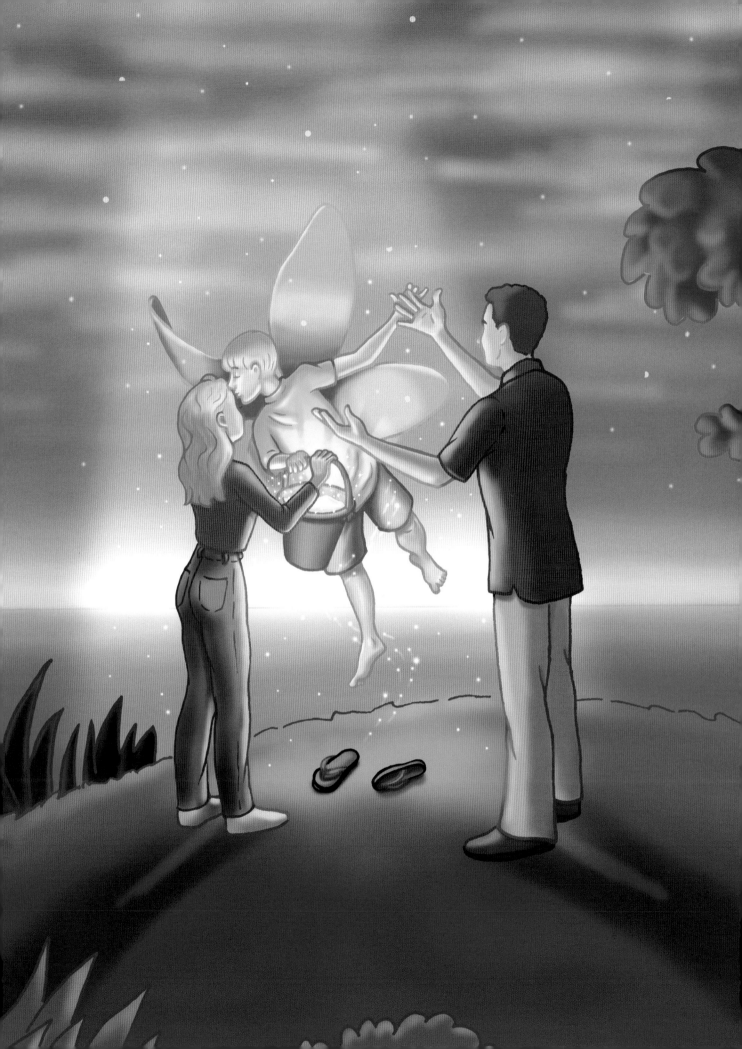

Then a beam of flickering lights descended and circled around them, only this time it swept Angelheart up to the heavens. Angelheart's parents waved good-bye, and blew him lots of kisses. They watched as he wrote a message for them in a trail of stars across the sky. Finally, after a very long time, they smiled. The message was complete. It said, "With Me Always, Angelheart".

Look up. Some of Angelheart's trail of stars can still be seen today. You might know it by a different name. It's called the Milky Way.

The Heavenly End